Our National Experience,

The Great American Cliché

by Lawrence Paros

★★★★

Workman Publishing Co., New York

wherever fine books are sold

Library of Congress Cataloging in Publication Data
Paros, Lawrence.
  The great American cliché.

  I. Title.
PN6162.P34   818'.5'407   75-44410

Design by Stephen Logowitz, with assistance from Jane Dickson
Edited by Jan Sharpless
Cover design by Paul Hanson

Workman Publishing Company, Inc.
231 East 51 Street
New York, New York 10022

Manufactured in The Good Ole U.S. of A.
First printing, March 1976
1 2 4 6 8 9 7 5 3

Acknowledgments:

Let me be the first to acknowledge my shortcomings: a debt of gratitude to my wise mentor; my many distinguished colleagues; my students from whom I have learned so much; the typist (hardworking, never complained) who in addition to the preparation of the manuscript, offered encouragement and criticism. My wife, long-suffering, prepared the index.

A special word of thanks to all-of-you-out-there and especially you-know-who. The errors and shortcomings, of course, are my own, or words to that effect.

THIS BOOK IS

Ordinary people just like you and me. People on the go. People from all walks of life. People who need people.

All power to the people!

DEDICATED TO

Milling crowds. Massive throngs. Teeming thousands. Saying what they please. Speaking their minds. Talking straight. Telling it like it is. The long and short of it.

Good evening
Mr. and Mrs. North and South America
and
All the ships at sea

. . . Let's go to press!

The Fourteen Points*

*The Good Lord himself had only ten.
Clemenceau

But first,
a word from
our sponsor . . .

Tired of the everyday grind?

Ever dream of a life of romantic adventure?

Want to get away from it all?

Return
with us
to the thrilling
days of
yesteryear

Come to where
the action is
God's Country
Land of the free
Home of the brave
Cradle of liberty
Famous for quality
since 1776

Known for its
Clean-cut youth
Solid citizens
Loyal Americans

For God and country
From all of us
To all of you
A warm welcome
A big hello

Y'all have a good time now, ya hear

We now return to tonight's epic saga:

THE AMERICAN WAY
OUR NATION'S STORY

Through word of mouth

To coin a phrase
To borrow an old cliché
When you've heard one, you've heard them all

CHAPTER I

America's Childhood

OR

It seems like only yesterday

The Birth of a Nation
The Origin of Species

It all begins with a friendly kiss

I've got something to tell you
Nothin' says lovin' like somethin' from the oven
There's a sucker born every minute
A little bundle of joy
A gift from heaven
Good things come in small packages
And baby makes three

Today is the first day of the rest of your life

A crying
need

Did

baby

have

A star is born
Kitchey-koo
How's the little one?
My, how you've grown
Like a weed
What do you want to be when you grow up?
This is America
Where any boy can grow up to be president

an accident?

Whatsamatter?
Cat got your tongue?

Eat your heart out!

Open wide, here comes the steam shovel
Amen, and pass the peas
Man does not live by bread alone

What's eating you?

Think of the starving children in India

Don't you want to grow
up to be big and strong?

Be a good little soldier and finish everything on your plate

All gone!

Little man, you've had a busy day

Time to go to bed

Beddy-bye

You have to get up pretty

early in the morning to fool

Your old man

Mommy,
get me
a drink
of water

"Daddy, tell me a story"

A Human
Interest
Story

No, he can't go out and play today. Caught with his hand in the cookie jar. Having more than one. Caught red-handed. A *prima facie* case. Guilt written all over his face. ★ What do you mean jellybean? I am not a crook. I'm clean as a hound's tooth. No tell-tale traces. I cannot tell a lie. HE did it. And that's the story, morning glory. ★ I'll get to the bottom of this. If it's the last thing I do. Don't open up a mouth like that to your mother! Wait 'til your father gets home. Prepare to meet your maker. You're gonna get it! I wash my hands of you!

Justice must be
served
The guilty must
suffer
Those responsible
must
be made to pay

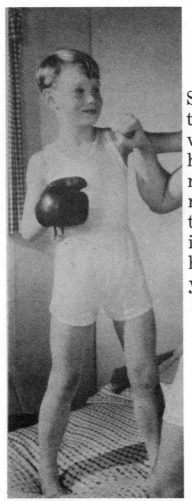

Son,
this
will
hurt
me
more
than
it
hurts
you

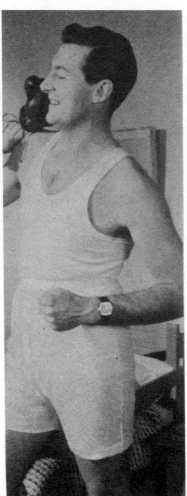

That's what they all say
You don't love me anymore
You're out to get me
Always pickin' on me
I'm gonna run away
You'll be sorry

You won't have Dick Nixon
to kick around anymore

That spells
fini
Curtains
Lights-out
Nighty-night

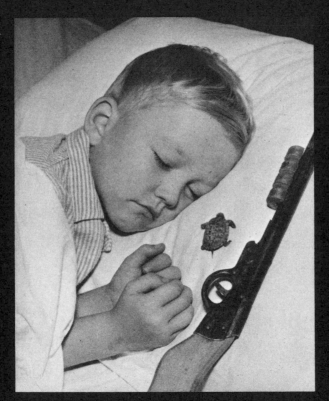

Don't let the bedbugs bite

CHAPTER II

America Goes to School

OR

As the twig is bent

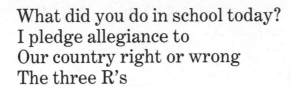

What did you do in school today?
I pledge allegiance to
Our country right or wrong
The three R's

Show and Tell
What I did on my summer vacation
Run Spot, Run!
Only with a note from your mother

Good morning children!
I'm going to teach you a thing or two
A lesson you won't forget
When you get older, you'll thank me for it

Let's get a few things straight
Name, date, and homeroom in the upper right hand corner
One inch margins
You've got to draw the line somewhere

The most important lesson of all

Discipline is the cornerstone of the educational process

★ A State of Military Preparedness
   Spare the rod
   If you let one of them get away with it
   Spoils the barrel
   Ruins it for everyone

★ Pre-emptive Strike
   Get your fuckin' hands offa me

★ Pacification
   No talking
   Eyes front
   One at a time

★ Protective reaction
   You there!

★ Escalation
   Not all at once
   Keep it down to a dull roar
   Repeat after me
   The whole class suffers

★ De-escalation
   I'll pretend I didn't hear that

Don't get smart with me

I go by the book
Books are your
friends

With friends like that, who needs enemies?

Open your books

Who can tell me the answer?
Raise your hands
Reach
The head of the class
No telling how far a bright boy like you can go

A tough act to follow
Johnny-on-the-spot

The Guidance Counselor

Come in son
My door is always open
A confidential chat

There's nothing like an education
Expand your horizons
Make something of yourself
Doctor, Lawyer, Indian Chief
Pay your dues
You can't get anywhere without a degree
You better believe it
It's your ticket
Your passport
Learn baby, learn!

Why Johnny can't read

Disadvantaged
A broken home
Cavity-prone
A dose of the Clap
The heartbreak of psoriasis
You've got to watch him every minute
Threatens the very foundation of a free society

Need I say more?

Where you comin' from man?
Where you at?

Maybe you'd
be happier
in the general
course?

The Bad Kid

Bad apple
Bad egg
Born loser
Problem child
Rebel without a cause
He'll never amount to anything
Send this kid to camp
Send for his mother
This is for your own good
Can't you do anything right?
Underachiever
Heredity or environment?
Going through a phase
Not working up to capacity
Not realizing his potential

Where did we go wrong?

The Good Kid

Why can't you be like him?
Most likely to succeed
In a class by himself
From a good family
Well above the national norm
High marks
Pride in personal appearance
25% fewer cavities
Perfect attendance
I enjoyed having him in homeroom this year
Works well with others
A good citizen
Blackboard monitor
Latin club treasurer
National Honor Society
Boys' State
Lav Patrol

All the tools,
but more important,
the right attitude

POMP AND CIRCUMSTANCE

Mortar-boards and sheepskins
Bright-eyed, bushy-tailed
The world awaits you

A
bright
future
ahead

A
rendezvous
with
destiny

CHAPTER III

America Comes of Age*

★★★★★★★★★★★★★★★★★★★★★

★ Positive identification required
Mature subject matter
Parental discretion advised

For openers
Boy meets girl

All-American

The girl-next-door

A sweet young thing

Pure (99 44/100%) as the driven snow

Sugar and spice

Peaches and cream

Blue-eyed blonde

Sweetheart of Sigma Chi

Girl

In *this* corner:
Mr. Right
Knight on a white charger
Prince Charming
That daring and resourceful
masked rider of the plains
A man's man
A man who has everything
Man, oh Manischewitz!
A he-man
Tall, dark, and handsome
Well-hung
Make no mistake about that

America's Sweetheart

Just like the girl that married dear old dad

The girl of my dreams

I'd like you to meet my folks

Pleased ta meetcha

Heaven help
The working girl

A girl's got to think about her reputation
Have you ever done it?
Mind your P's and Q's
The facts of life
Your privates
The birds and the bees
Our Judaeo-Christian heritage

A word to the wise
The rules of the road
If you want them to respect you
In a pinch
Let him down gently
Call for help

Rally for decency!
Put God in your heart
Accompanied by an adult
Be Good
Or else be careful
The National Safety Council says
Don't take it lying down
Don't stay out too late

Don't wait up for us!

The
Dating
Game

A body-contact sport
Ball One!

Make your pitch
I want to hold your hand
Russian hands and Roman fingers
Me Tarzan, You Jane
If I told you you had a great body
Would you hold it against me?
Cotton, wool, or felt?
You show me yours, and I'll show you mine

What will the neighbors say?

Not on the first

Oh come on baby!
Where've you been?
You'll never catch a man that way

date. What do you take me for? Are your intentions honorable? I'm not that kind of girl.

Promise her anything, but give her An idea whose time has come.
So near, and yet so far. STRUCK OUT! That's the way the cookie crumbles. Such is life.

Crude, Rude, and Socially-Unattractive. Couple of guys out for a couple of laughs. Hey guys, wait up! Watcha wanna do tonight? I dunno, whatchoo wanna do? Get laid. ★ How's your love life? Gettin' much? Here and there. Find 'em, Feel 'em, Fuck'em And Forget 'em.

Bottom's Up!

Meanwhile, back at the ranch . . .

I see London, I see France. Love at first sight. A real eyeful. I'm just a girl who can't say no. The Sexual Revolution. Whatever turns you on. Let it all hang out. Let the good times roll. ★ Our finest hour. Going all the way. Wham, Bamm, Thank you Ma'am. I like it, I like it. And one for good luck. ★ Having a wonderful time. Wish you were here. Enjoyed having you. Come again. ★ Keep in touch.

CHAPTER IV

America
at Home

★ ★ ★ ★ ★ ★ ★ ★ ★ ★ ★

The house is a mess,
but come on in!

For better or for worse

HOT WATER
is a family affair

True love
His and hers
Marriage and the family
The cornerstone of
 our society
The solemn contract
Made in heaven
The bond of matrimony
Two consenting adults
Tied the knot
Really tied one on

The blushing bride
　Something borrowed,
　something blue

Blue Monday
Blue Cheer
Post-Partem Blues
True Blue

The honeymoon
　is over

Keep the homefires
burning

Home
sweet home

Where the
heart is

Where I
hang my hat

A nice place
to visit,
but I wouldn't
want to live there.

H-e-e-e-r-e's

The little woman. The better half. The happy homemaker. A great little cook. Neat as a pin. The quicker-picker-upper. Filling the needs of a growing America.

Let's have a big hand for the little lady

Actress, Mother, Cover-girl. This is your life.

Congestion
Tired blood
Post-nasal drip
Dull, lifeless hair
Tension-headache
Occasional acid indigestion and heartburn
Minor arthritic pain
You're only as old as you feel

My girdle is killing me

The hand that rocks the cradle

Up in arms

If you can't
stand the heat,
get out of the
kitchen

The
silent
partner.

This is your captain speaking
The head of the household
The male of the species

Now hear this
A good provider
Brings home the bacon
The bread-winner
A household word
The name you can trust
For a sure tomorrow

Hail to the chief

Knows his stuff
Knows what's what
You know what I mean?

Do you read me?
Father knows best
He's the man to see
In any organization,
it's the man at the top
who must assume the responsibility
I leave those decisions to my wife

The social amenities

The best to you each morning
Homecoming festivities
Did you have a good day at the office, dear?
Whata day   I'm beat   Whatsnew?
Whatsfersupper?

If you knew you were going to
be late, why didn't you call?

The games people play
Nag   Nag   Nag
If that don't beat all!

Get your house in order
Don't forget to take out the garbage

Honey, it seems like
we just don't talk to
each other anymore

A real life story. With a happy ending. The events are true. The names have

The Energy Crisis
I'm just too tired tonight, dear
Too pooped to pop Had my hair done today
Night out with the boys
I'm working late again at the office
The other woman
A little on the side

Can this
marriage
be saved?

Never say die
Make it work
Stay together
for the kids' sake

I never promised
you a rose garden
It takes a heap lot o' livin'
to make a
house a home

Tender
loving care
And they lived
happily ever after

All's well
that ends well

Have a nice day!

been changed to protect the innocent.

The best years of my life
How could you?
The house divided
The Union dissolved

The moral
of the story
The cardinal
principle

The family
that plays together
stays together
(Position in life
is everything)

CHAPTER V

America Comes Clean and Stays Healthy

★★★★★★★★★★★★★★★★★★★★★

OR

Don't you wish everybody did?

Five o'clock
shadow
(The Shadow
knows)

Join
the War on
Dirt.

Every litter bit hurts
Take aim against cavities
Eliminate offensive body odor
And Ring-Around-the-Collar
Hunt bugs down like radar
and kill them dead
Kill germs by millions on contact

A clean sweep
A total wipe-out

Don't forget to wash behind your ears

Cleanliness is next to godliness

Bare your soul

Make a clean breast of it

America
the beautiful
Drives out dirt
Stamps out smut
Attacks greasy smears

Blots on justice
Sordid scandals
Tough stains
On the highest office in the land

Dirty money
Laundered clean

A washday miracle
Hooray for the red, white, and blue!
Colors look even cleaner and brighter than before

Shit, shower, shave, and shampoo
An approved program of dental care

The Body Politic *or* Is there a doctor in the house? Take off your clothes, the doctor will be right with you. And how are we today. A cancer growing on the Presidency. We'll have you on your feet in no time. ★ A healthy America is a strong America. Lance the nation's sores. Bind the nation's wounds. Get America moving again. Get back in the swing. Get a gentle, mild laxative. Cleans clogged drains quickly. All systems are GO. Too young to go? That's what they all say.

SPEAKING of headaches . . . Do you know where your children are? Kids, you do for them your whole life: And what do you get? The Youth Problem. The Generation Gap. Drug Abuse, Public Enemy #1. Stoned. Strung-out. These kids don't know what they're doing to themselves. Reefer Madness. Leads to the hard stuff. The long term physical effects are not yet known. The Weed of Crime bears bitter fruit. Get high on America.

You're the doctor!
Take two every hour and call me in the morning

Just what the doctor ordered
One before dinner
A nightcap
One for the road
No thanks, I'm trying to cut down
Weeell, maybe just one
I can quit anytime I want to
I'll drink to that!

CHAPTER VI

America Works and Succeeds:

☆Part I☆

OR

This time we mean Business!

The Business
of America
is Business

Idle hands
are the devil's
plaything

Keep your nose
to the grindstone
Ear to the ground

Shoulder
to the wheel

Sunny side up

Whistle while you work

The dignity of labor
The Monday morning blahs
Another day, another dollar
A hard day's work for a good day's pay
A little hard work never hurt anyone

TGIF
The eagle shits
Three glorious days of fun in the sun
A little R & R
Under the Florida sunshine tree

Rugged Individualism. When my father first came to this country. He came up the hard way. Humble origins. Modest circumstances. Knew what it meant to be poor. Worked hard for what he got. 99% perspiration, 1% inspiration.

Down and out? Up and at 'em.

Up by your own bootstraps.

The bottom line.

God helps those who help themselves.

The Welfare state
With charity for all
A state of mind
Beggars all description
There is no such thing
as demeaning work!

Everybody has to start someplace.

The Self-Made Man:

The American Dream
Land of opportunity
Something for everyone
Every man a King
You only go around once
Reach high
Hitch your wagon to a star
Climb every mountain
Snatch the brass ring
Wear the mantle of success
Rags to riches
The top banana
Another fine product
Straight out of Horatio Alger
Made of stern stuff

Batteries not included

Ladies and Gentlemen
I AM A DEAF MUTE
I AM SELLING THIS CARD TO
SEE MY WAY THROUGH

My Prayer For You Is
May God Bless You
PAY ANY PRICE YOU WISH

Thank You   Good Luck

Nothing succeeds like success
Look out for Number One
We try harder
Local boy makes good
Lifted from obscurity
A meteoric rise
Dizzying heights
The pinnacle of success

Last one up is a rotten egg!

BUY AMERICAN

Be a credit to your people. Let me count the ways. Six easy installments. An equal opportunity lender. As close as your phone.

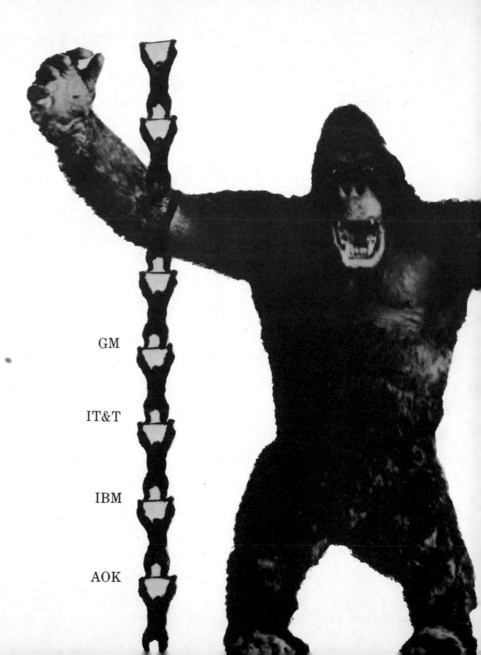

Take stock
in America

You can
bank on it

GM

Invest in
your future

IT&T

IBM

AOK

What's good for General Motors is good for the country

Progress is our most important product

Large, Jumbo, Super, King-size, Large economy size

Mammoth, Colossal

The   bigger   the   better

Caution:
Use only
as directed

We interrupt this program to bring you . . . **CHAPTER VII**

An importa

Strike a blow for freedom

Manifest Destiny

The American Way
Honor it
Defend it
Extend it

nt message

Sock it
to 'em

Proof through the night that our flag was still there

CARELESS MATCHES
AID THE AXIS

U S

CHAPTER VIII

And now the second half of

America Works and Succeeds:

OR

The impossible takes a little longer

Don't call us, we'll call you. You work, you struggle, you fight to survive. One day you look up, and — Sorry about that kid.

Good help is hard to find. Those are the breaks. That's show biz. Not an easy decision. I just work here. I don't make the rules.

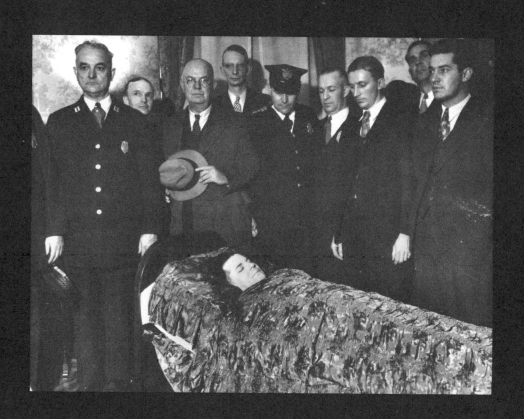

Your credit record is one of your most prized possessions

Go for broke
Sign on the dotted line

FOB

COD

SOB

SOS

IOU

Your payment is past due
Many happy returns of the day

Local color
That Old Black Magic
There goes the neighborhood

The economy sags. The ranks of the unemployed swell. Stocks plummet. Prices soar. Feeling the pinch. Sam, you made the pants too long, the jacket too tight.

Spiraling inflation, Public Enemy #1. Stretch the dollar. The shrinking dollar. Doesn't go as far as it used to. Funny money. No laughing matter. Brother, can you spare a dime? ★ Knock, knock, who's there? The wolf is at the door. Keep the faith baby. Cool it. It's always darkest before the dawn. Relief is just a swallow away. Prosperity is just around the corner.

The number
you have reached
is not a
working number

CHAPTER IX

America at Play

★ ★ ★ ★ ★ ★ ★ ★ ★ ★ ★

OR

Nice Guys Finish Last

TD's ERA's RBI's

Cliff-hangers   Squeakers

   Seat-squirmers   Game-savers

Hitting the long jump shot at the buzzer   Splitting the
                                                  uprights with
                                                  only seconds
                                                  remaining

                                        Tennis, anyone?

The thrill of victory. The agony of defeat. Be a good sport. Do some-

thing — anything! If you can't be an athlete, be an athletic supporter. An

armchair quarterback. In the comfort of your livingroom.

KO's and DP's

More than just a game

Builds character
The lesson that stays with you all your life
Winner take all
That's the name of the game
The thing that made us great
The killer instinct
The free enterprise system

Molder of character

Let me make one thing perfectly clear
The Fundamentals
United we stand, divided we fall
A team effort
Shoulder to shoulder
Cheek to jowl
Every man pulling together
Giving their all

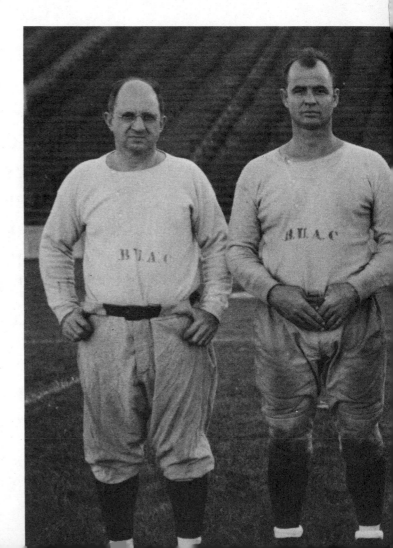

... maker of men

Running a team is not a popularity contest
He got that something extra out of us
I learned more from him in that one year . . .
I love his ass

I'd run over my grandmother for him

The very good looking
young ballplayer

Strapping, raw-boned

God-given ability

All the ingredients
That something extra
Talent to burn

The steady
day-in,
day-out
performer

A money ballplayer
The Kid
The seasoned veteran
The old pro
Down for the count
Branded a loser
The experts said
Washed up
I'm afraid your playing days are over
The long road back
An uphill struggle all the way
Comeback of the year
A game fighter
SPUNK
Desire was his middle name

THE

The Superbowl. The United States of America vs. The President of all the people. A classic encounter.

A must game.   Going for all the marbles.

BIG

The match-up all America has been waiting for.
Everything riding on this one.

The pennant.   The trophy.
The flag.   The title.

GAM

A tense drama in the making. Under a broiling noonday sun. A full house. SRO.
Packed to the rafters.
Rhythmic chants.
Deafening cheers.

On the edge of their collective seats.

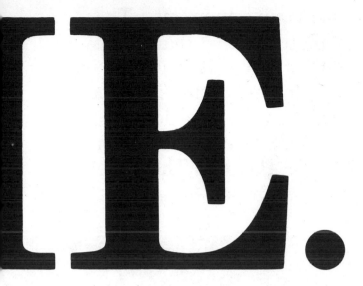

When push comes to shove
Remember the game plan
Dig in
Tough it out
Grapple with your problems
Wrestle with your conscience

Don't jump to conclusions
When the going gets tough, the tough get going
Get what I mean?
Now get out there
Win this one for the Gipper

Down to the Wire. How time flies. The waning moments. That just about puts the game on ice. ★ Don't touch that dial. The game isn't over until the last man is out. ★ Hold the phone. Hold everything. The moment you've all been waiting for. The old statue-of-liberty play. A brilliant display of open-field running. Daylight ahead. Clear sailing. The light at the end of the tunnel. Land ho! Good old terra-firma. Paydirt. The sweet smell of success.

When
the
cheering
stopped

Congratulations are in order
Mazel Tov
Thanks but no thanks
It's all in the wrists
Everything that I am and ever will be
I owe to . . .
Practice, exercise and
The Breakfast of Champions
Two of the finest public servants
it has ever been my privilege to know
I couldn't have done it by myself
I just don't know what to say at a time like this
God bless us everyone
A sports immortal
A legend in his own time
A dream come true
I dreamt about this ever since I was a little kid
World Champ-een
of these United States

Son, wake up!
You must have had a bad dream
Our long national nightmare is over

CHAPTER X

America Keeps the Peace

A whodunit
Soon to be made into a major motion picture

66 We came in peace. One giant leap for mankind. To make the world safe for democracy. To win the hearts and minds of the people. **99**

Search and destroy. Huns, Jerries, Nips, Cockeyed Ladrones. Johnny Rebs, Redskins. The Yellow Peril. Redcoats, Reds, Dinks, and Charlies. The Lunatic Fringe. The Enemies List.

We will bury you
The Communist master plan for world domination
Better Red than Dead?
I'd rather fight than switch
America, Bastion of Democracy, Hope of the Free World

Conspiracy
Behind the Iron Curtain
The Enemy Within
They are after the hearts and minds of your children
Keep a close eye out!

Are you now or have you ever been a
Commie dupe, Nervous Nellie, Peacenik
Nattering nabob of negativism
Effete intellectual
Impudent snob

Honk
if you
love
Jesus!

The Domino Theory:

Don't
fall
for
it.

The Lesson
of Munich

Be prepared

Speak softly,
and carry a
big stick

Hit 'em where
they ain't

Remember the Alamo. Remember the Maine.

Quemoy and Matsu? Where are they now?   Ninety miles off our shore

Care enough
to send the
very best

Greetings

Uncle Sam wants you

I never met a man I didn't like

The Selective Service System

Old-Fashioned draft style flavor

The special feeling, the special pride that comes with wearing the uniform

The Army Way

Good morning men
Good morning sergeant
I can't hear you
Good morning sergeant

I give the orders around here
Knock off the horseplay
Keep your eyes, ears,
and bowels open,
and your mouth closed
Loose lips sink ships
I need three volunteers:
You, you, and you
Tell it to the Marines
Such loyalty won't go unrewarded

'Nam. Where it's at. The right to choose their own destiny. An offer they can't refuse. They should only live so long.

We had to destroy the village
in order to save it. What on earth?
Who's in charge here? Who me? I
didn't see a thing.

Stick to your guns. Peace with honor. Saving face.
Winding down. Turning the corner. Ringing

down

the

curtain.

The most unpopular war in U.S. History

All over but the shouting

Quoth the raven, Nevermore

COME BACK SOON

and bring
the kids

CHAPTER XI

America Keeps the Law

Thank God we don't live in a police state

The law of the land
The ground-rules

A government of laws and not of men
No man above the law
No man a law unto himself
For that very special occasion
Dirty tricks   Covert operations
Everyone's doing it
Factory-authorized
Don't make a federal case out of it

A fair trial
A jury of your peers
With justice for all

Different strokes for different folks
For our regular customers
A lifetime guarantee

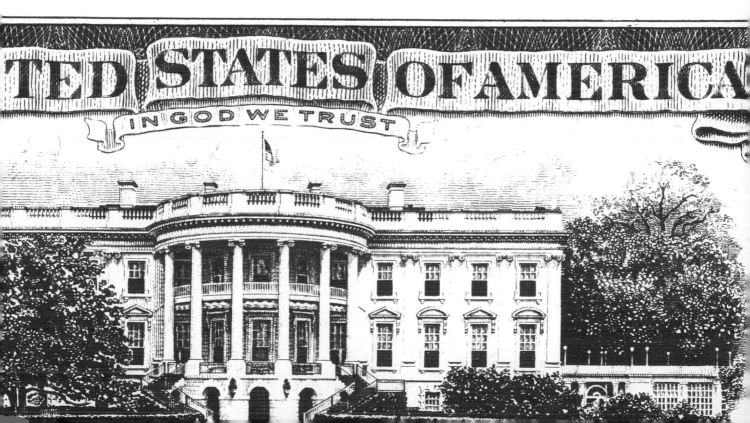

The majority rules
The majority is always right
Any number can play

The Big Three
The Awesome Front Four
The Jackson Five
The Economical Six-Pack
The Chicago Seven
The eight essential vitamins & iron
The Catonsville Nine
The Milwaukee Fourteen
The Top 40
The Indianapolis 500

The proper
psychological moment

The moment of truth
has arrived

It's time to play . . .

To tell the truth. You bet your life. This court is now in session. Heah come da judge. Order in the court-room. First one to talk is a monkey's uncle. The law requires that I inform you of your rights. Your right to remain silent. Your last chance to beat the other couple. No help from the audience, please. There will be no outbursts while I'm on the bench. I am the law out here. Just do as I say and you won't get hurt.

truth or consequences

Approach the bench. Belly up to the bar, boys. Watch it! One false step and it could be your last. Motion denied. Objection! Counsel is leading the witness. Overruled! After all, what are friends for? Say the secret word and split $100 between you. I respect-fully decline to answer on grounds that. I've got a secret. Not suitable for persons under the age of 21. A clear and present danger. Without redeeming social value. Let's retire to my chambers.

What's my line?
Take the fifth
Stonewall the jury
Beat the rap
Anything you say can be held against you
Name, rank, and serial number
To make a long story short

                            Let's make a deal
            Easy terms are available
                            Cop a plea
        Buy some time

                                    The price is right

                I retain my faith in the American jury system
        Don't knock it 'til you've tried it

There oughta be a law!

Much ado about nothing. The right to life movement. Ban the bomb. Make love, not war. Draft beer, not students. Dump the Hump. Phoo on Nhu. Public Enemy #1. (You can say that again.) Outside Agitators. Outside the law. The source of urban unrest. The long hot summer. Campus violence. Listen, kiddo. I was fighting Nazis before you were born. When you've seen one, you've seen them all. The Bill of Rights wasn't meant to include THEM. Rights are earned. In *our* America.

Now take me. Some of my best friends are. Middle-Americans. Hard-hats. Members of the silent majority. Working stiffs. Decent, god-fearing folk. Dear hearts and gentle people. The forgotten American. The little guy. The slob who broke his ass for this country. That's what this country is really all about.

Ballots not bullets. Lawful means to effect desired change. Every major independent poll shows. Change does not come overnight. Violence never proves anything.

Don't coddle criminals. These times call for special measures. I thought I'd get me one. Bang, bang, you're dead! Brush your teeth and go to bed.

Have gun will travel. Chicago, Chicago, that toddlin'
town. Give us this day our daily bread. Shoot to kill. Shoot
on sight. Shoot first, ask questions later. The right of
every American to bear arms. Register Communists, not
guns. When guns are outlawed only outlaws will have
guns. The Saturday night special. The Saturday massacre.
Crime in the streets. Hazardous to your health.
Chicago's finest.
The boys in blue.
Let you get a good
night's sleep.

CHAPTER XII
WE PAUSE NOW FOR STATION IDENTIFICATION

This is America
The Great White Way
Address of the stars
Home of
Your tired, your poor, your
Spics, Greasers, Dagos, Crackers,
Kikes, Wops, Polaks,
Bluebloods, Rednecks,
Chinks, Micks, Wasps, Frogs,
Greaseballs, Niggers,
Pushy Jews, and Gooks

The melting pot
The crucible
E pluribus unum
Strength in diversity
Viva la difference!
57 different varieties
Accept no substitutes
A wide selection
Americans all

But would you want
your sister to marry one?

Our thought for today:

One nation under God
Count yourself in
Consider yourself one of the family

Glad to be aboard
What did you say your name was?
Funny, you don't look
Afro-American
Call a spade a spade

Bridge the gaps of generation and race
Bring us together again
Without regard to race, sex, creed, or national origin
With all deliberate speed

CHAPTER XIII

America Governs Itself

OR

What you see is what you get

DEMOCRATIC NOMINEES

FOR PRESIDENT

FOR VICE PRESIDENT

WHAT WE STAND BY.

TARIFF REFORM.
WAR TAXES MUST CEASE.
NO TREASURY SURPLUS.
ECONOMIC ADMINISTRATION.
EQUAL RIGHTS TO ALL.
LABOR PROTECTION.
FREEDOM FROM MONOPOLY AND CLASS LEGISLATION.
A JUST USE OF TAX PAYERS' MONEY.
ECONOMY IN PUBLIC EXPENSE.
NO RINGS OF GRAFT.
HONEST ADMINISTRATION.
PRESERVATION.

GROVER CLEVELAND.   OUR CHOICE.   A. G. THURMAN.

What have *they* done for you lately?

Politics American style
Tomorrow's promises today
Fair deal   Square deal   New deal
Dirty deal
Dealt out
Lost in the shuffle

A trip down
memory lane

Normalcy
The Crash
Tippecanoe and Tyler too
How soon they forget
The commiecrat party of
betrayal
Creeping socialism
The welfare mess
The Grand Old Party
The party of Lincoln
Not a cough in a carload

That brief moment
that was Camelot
The New Frontier
The Great Society
A chicken in every pot
A car in every garage
40 acres and a mule
Promises, promises
Fish your wish
Throw the rascals out

The faith of our fathers

The two party system. Shirts or skins. Steer a middle course. Moderation in all things. Nine out of ten doctors surveyed agree that. My dog's better than your dog. Two sides to every question. It's a free country. Which side are you on?

Get to know
America

To know her is to love her. The people's right to know. In the national interest. Classified. Top Secret. Eyes Only. No Comment. What you don't know won't hurt you. The walls have ears. A little knowledge is a dangerous thing.

Legitimate beefs. Write your congressman. Right

on. Keep those cards and letters coming. I'm glad

you asked that. I've just appointed a presidential

fact-finding commission. A blue-ribbon panel of

distinguished citizens. Each a leading authority in

his field. And away go problems down the drain.

Don't Throw in the Towel
You can't fight city-hall
It isn't what you know,
but who you know
Smoke-filled rooms
Cost-overruns
Special favors
Tax loopholes
Obstruction of justice
Nobody's perfect!

What'll you have?

Not just another pretty face
The Real Thing

Famous last words

Yes and No
Sort of, but not really
Fish or cut bait
Shit or get off the pot
Take the bull by the horns
Look him squarely in the eye
It's a once in a lifetime opportunity

To return the unused portion

The System works.
The genius and wisdom of the founding fathers.
The machinery of state goes on.

We're on the thres

(Expletive deleted)

(Weigh it carefully)

| The pound of flesh | Let bygones be bygones | Forgive and forget | Close ranks |

hold of a new era.

Let us
go forward
together

A whole
new ballgame

A clean
slate

Wish us
luck!

CHAPTER XIV

Whither America?

After all is said and done

Food for thought

All hell to pay

Endangered species

Deep in debt

High in saturated fats

Water, water, everywhere

and not a drop to drink

All good things must come to an end
The party's over
The times they are a-changin'
Which way out?

Yo**U**th wants to know

Whither
America?

That about wraps it up

The shape of the world today

The Forecast for Tomorrow:

Occasional sunshine

Menacing clouds on the horizon

A nine out of ten chance of

The shit hitting the fan

All past statements are now inoperative

And that's the way it is